Victorian Watercolours

CHILDREN

Victorian Watercolours
CHILDREN

ADRIAN VINCENT

Bloomsbury Books
London

There is a wealth of Victorian watercolours available. Many were painted by artists who only produced a few paintings and little of their personal history is known. For this reason, it has not always been possible to find out the date of birth and death for all the artists shown in this book. 'Exhibited' gives the dates when an artist's work is known to have appeared in exhibitions. 'Flourished' gives the dates for the main body of an artist's work.

First published in Great Britain 1987 by Michael Joseph Ltd.
© 1987 Beanstalk Books Ltd.
Produced by Beanstalk Books Ltd.
This edition published 1991 by Bloomsbury Books
an imprint of Godfrey Cave Associates Limited
42 Bloomsbury Street, London WC1B 3QJ
under license from Beanstalk Books Ltd.

ISBN 1-8547-1021-4

Designed by Lee Robinson

British Library Cataloguing in Publication Data

Vincent, Adrian
    Children. – (Victorian watercolours).
    1. Watercolor painting, British 2. Water-
    color painting, Victorian – Great Britain
    3. Children in art
    I. Title II. Series
    757'.5'0941   ND2202.G7

Printed in Great Britain by Eagle Colourbooks Ltd.

Acknowledgements
The assistance of the following art dealers, auctioneers and the Royal Academy in lending colour photographs for this book is gratefully acknowledged.

Bourne Gallery
31 Lesbourne Rd,
Reigate,
Surrey RH2 7JS.

J. Collins & Son
The Studio,
63 and 28 High St,
Bideford,
Devon EX39 2AN.

Fine-Lines (Fine Art)
The Old Rectory,
31 Ship St,
Shipston on Stour,
Warwick CV36 4AE.

Anthony Mitchell Fine Paintings
Sunnymede House,
11 Albemarle Rd,
Woodthorpe,
Nottingham NG5 4FE.

Phillips (Auctioneers)
Blenstock House,
7 Blenheim St,
New Bond St,
London W1Y 0AS.

The Priory Gallery
The Priory, Station Rd,
Bishops Cleeve,
Cheltenham, Glos.

The Royal Academy
Piccadilly,
London W1V 0DS.

The Weald Gallery
Southdown House,
The High St,
Brasted,
Nr. Sevenoaks, Kent.

Contents

GEORGE GOODWIN KILBURNE

1839-1924

A well-known and extremely popular artist in his lifetime, George Goodwin Kilburne was one of those hard-working Victorian painters who found time not only to exhibit regularly at all the major galleries, but also to make regular contributions as a book and magazine illustrator. Examples of his work appeared in the *Graphic* and the greatly respected *Cornhill Magazine*.

Born in Norfolk on 24 July 1839, he started his professional career as an apprentice engraver for the Dalziel brothers, with whom he stayed for six years. Thereafter he turned to watercolour painting, specialising in genre pictures, many of which depicted eighteenth-century courting couples. His large output of costume pieces became so popular that many were made into prints. He was really more at ease recreating contemporary scenes where his work achieved a sense of reality never found to the same degree in his period pieces. A regular exhibitor at the Royal Academy for more than fifty years, he still had time to pursue his favourite hobby of collecting arms and armour.

Kilburne's watercolour, *Blind Man's Bluff*, is typical of his work. It is a lively and charming study of a Victorian children's party, in which the holly and mistletoe reveal that it is Christmas. The Christmas season evoked a sentimental response from many Victorians and this, combined with charming children, were ingredients bound to ensure the picture's popularity.

For the children in Kilburne's painting, nothing equalled the joys of Christmas, its impending arrival heralded first by Papa coming home with the tree, and then by the flood of Christmas cards landing on the door mat. Henry Cole, the first director of the Victoria and Albert Museum, must be credited with the invention of the Christmas card in 1843, the same year that Charles Dickens's *A Christmas Carol* arrived in the bookshops.

There were many excitements to look forward to; putting up the Christmas decorations, the sight of cook returning from the butcher's with an enormous goose, and perhaps a glimpse of Papa surreptitiously entering the house laden with mysterious parcels.

On Christmas Eve children hung up their stockings – another Victorian idea – and awoke the next morning to find them veritable cornucopiae of toys. For those Victorian children fortunate enough to belong to the monied classes, protected by their background from the want and sometimes destitution which beset their poorer counterparts, Christmas was indeed a delightful time with presents and plum pudding, much family jollity and, for the lucky ones, a visit to the theatre.

Blind Man's Bluff
Courtesy The Priory Gallery

ROSE MAYNARD BARTON

1856-1929

Few Victorian women seemed attracted to painting in oils but this was not true of watercolour painting, an area where many flourished, even exhibiting in the London galleries, though none of them achieved quite the same fame as Helen Allingham. These women represent a small army of painters whose work made a valuable contribution to the art of the period. One reason for their success in this field was that they dealt with gallery owners, a group less prejudiced against women painters than the average member of the public, who might have felt reluctant to buy a painting directly from a woman, perhaps sensing something unseemly in such a rare and normally discouraged instance of female independence.

Rose Maynard Barton was one of the more popular women artists. Born in Ireland on 21 April 1856, the daughter of a local solicitor, she left to study painting in Paris. Later she settled in London and began to exhibit regularly at all the major galleries including the Royal Academy, where seventeen of her pictures were shown. A talented landscape and genre painter, she is chiefly associated with foggy views of London. Children were always a favourite subject throughout the whole of her career, even though she never had any herself.

Rose Maynard Barton worked on two books. In 1898 she provided wash drawings for *Picturesque Dublin, Old and New*. She also wrote the text and painted watercolours for *Familiar London* in 1904.

Her watercolour, *Grandpa's Garden*, is a delightful example of her work. Although outrageously sentimental, its subject is so endearing and its colours so vibrant that only the most stony-hearted viewer could fail to warm to it. The gravity of the little child's bearing as she watches the Chelsea pensioner preparing her a nosegay is wonderfully observed.

The pensioner, who must have seen action in one of Queen Victoria's wars, perhaps in the Crimea, has been observed with the same perceptive eye which has frozen his slow, aged movements into a single moment. The garden, filled with sunflowers, roses, poppies, phlox, pansies and daisies, is surely one that even Helen Allingham would have envied, who had made her reputation by painting just such gardens. (See RURAL LIFE in the same series.)

This was a time when the country garden was in danger of extinction. In the eighteenth century, in large gardens it had become the fashion to replace the flower beds with lawn. In the small cottage garden, hard times forced the humble countryman to root out his plants and replace them with vegetables. The large garden filled with flowers did not make a comeback until the latter part of the nineteenth century when gardening writers began pleading for its return. This roughly coincided with an improvement in the farm worker's lot who, while keeping some of his vegetables, could restore his front garden to much of its former glory.

Grandpa's Garden
Courtesy The Priory Gallery

EDWARD KILLINGWORTH JOHNSON

1825-1896

Edward Killingworth Johnson was a self-taught artist who, although he had previously exhibited three pictures at the Royal Academy, did not take up painting as a profession until he was thirty-eight. In this respect he may be likened to Birket Foster, who always claimed that he had never had a serious art lesson in his life.

Johnson was born in Stratford-le-Bow in 1825 and gained popularity for his landscape and genre paintings in his lifetime. His work was particularly admired by Birket Foster who bought one of his watercolours, *The Anxious Mother*, in 1876. Unusually, for an English artist, Johnson's work was also well-known in America, where it was exhibited in New York.

Johnson was an artist whose output was always highly polished. His technique was unusual in its almost invariable combination of pure watercolour with body colour, a method whereby watercolour paints are mixed with white to render them opaque and give them substance. This practice aroused disapproval from purists in the earlier part of the century as such paint is liable to crack and flake off if applied too heavily. It is often referred to as gouache.

In 1871 Johnson moved from London to Halstead in Essex. He died on 7 April 1896 leaving behind him more than one hundred and ninety watercolours.

His watercolour, *Her First Sorrow*, is an excellent example of his highly-detailed style which deservedly brought him praise from critics and fellow artists alike. Every leaf, every blade of grass has been depicted with all the subtle gradations of colour that nature can achieve, caught with an exactitude rarely seen in watercolours. The same treatment has been applied to the girl's clothing; every crease of her dress is shown, each wrinkle in her stockings. Even her well-worn but good-quality leather shoes have been painstakingly executed. Bearing in mind the dedicated realism of the painter's approach, it is remarkable that he has not produced a purely mechanical painting (as can so often happen when a feel for the subject is sacrificed to the reproduction of near photographic detail); indeed, this picture is very much alive.

A young girl mourning a dead dove was the sort of subject calculated to please the Victorians, who had a morbid preoccupation with death, especially when children were involved. This was hardly surprising as every Victorian child was a potential victim of the twin evils of tuberculosis and diphtheria which were then rampant at every level of society.

Her First Sorrow
Courtesy Bourne Gallery

WILLIAM ALEXANDER

Flourished 1878-1898

William Alexander is best known for his land-scape scenes painted around his home town of Salisbury, but it is obvious from his water-colour, *The Young Master*, that he was also an accomplished figure artist. Although he exhibited regularly for twenty years, including works at the Royal Academy, he still remains one of those Victorian painters of whom little is known. If this seems strange, it must be remembered that the field is an enormous one. Art historians have already managed to unearth information on some seventy thousand artists, but there are still many who need to be researched. The Victorians took watercolour painting very seriously and many talented amateurs went to have lessons from professional watercolour artists.

Alexander's *The Young Master* is a marvellous example of watercolour painting. Countless hours must have been spent in achieving the almost photographic detail of every single element. The carving and basket weave on the back of the Gothic style chair, the shabby look of the artist's portfolio resting against the chair leg, even the picture on the bowl on the mantlepiece could have been caught by the lens of a good camera. However, only a painting could capture the depth between the potted plant and the wallpapered dado.

The 'young master' is attired in Scottish national dress, not because he was a young Scot, but because it had become the vogue to dress both boys and girls in tartan. This fashion had been set by Prince Albert and the young Prince of Wales who were seen in Highland dress during the rebuilding of Balmoral Castle in the mid 1850s. The attire looks charming in Alexander's painting. Unfortunately, many a hapless child became the victim of his mother's bad taste when she insisted that her young son's tartan dress be made more elaborate. Young boys were to be seen dressed in a tartan frock under a dark jacket, the whole attire surmounted by a huge feathered hat. Some mothers, with a misguided sense of prudery, even dressed their little boys with the kilt worn over a pair of short trousers!

The Young Master
Courtesy Bourne Gallery

AGNES GARDNER KING

Exhibited 1880-1902

Agnes Gardner King was a watercolour artist whose style and subject matter could just as easily have lent themselves to successful book illustration. Some of her paintings, such as *A Wee Scotch Lass*, *The Little Persian Pet*, and her picture here, *Beside the River*, would have been ideal for an annual such as *Little Folks*. Instead, she became a landscape, figure and flower artist who also specialised in painting miniatures.

A highly professional artist whose work was exhibited at all the major galleries, including the Royal Academy, it is probable that she would have achieved even higher regard had her genre work been less cloying. Her sister, Elizabeth Thomson King, with whom she lived in Florence, London and Newbury was also a landscape and figure artist.

Agnes King's watercolour, *Beside the River*, is typical of her painting and is an accomplished piece of work, even if one finds the sentimentality a little overdone. The picture is a large one, which probably entailed the artist adding glycerine to her water so that the washes could be manipulated more easily before they dried. This was a common practice with artists working in warm weather when the drying process was inevitably accelerated. The trees look realistic at first glance but in fact the washes have been applied in an Impressionistic manner. In direct contrast is the treatment of the girl and her lamb, which have been executed in a very detailed way, as have the wild irises. This deliberate mingling of styles reflects the artist's confidence. The use on the dress of Chinese White, first put on the market by Winsor & Newton in 1834, is particularly effective.

The subject matter, the little girl walking her lamb, bears as much relation to life as a character from a nursery rhyme. It might just as well have been entitled *Mary and her Little Lamb*, and was obviously painted entirely from the imagination. The piece exemplifies those twin myths of the Victorian age: that all little girls were sweet and saintly looking, and that there was no dark side to rural life.

This myth of rural comfort was perpetuated by a large number of Victorian writers supplying escapist literature for the urban Victorian wishing to withdraw a while from the pressure and dirt of city life. Even Thomas Hardy, himself a countryman, was guilty of this to some degree in *Under the Greenwood Tree*. Here he writes about likeable village musicians and singers, seemingly without a care in the world beyond the fear that they might be ousted from their jobs at the church at Mellstock by the arrival of a new village organ.

Indeed, town dwellers viewed countrymen as a race quite apart from themselves, even though no less than one person in every two lived in the country during the hey-day of Victoria's reign.

Beside the River
Courtesy Weald Gallery

HELENA MAGUIRE

1860-1909

Helena Maguire was born in 1860 and her work was directly influenced by such major water-colour artists as Birket Foster and William Henry Hunt, but she undoubtedly had creative ability of her own. This lay mostly in her sense of line and instinctive knowledge and use of colour. In respect of colour she benefited considerably from the fact that since the mid 1840s an almost bewildering array of colours had become available to the artist in metal tubes.

She was the daughter of Thomas Herbert Maguire, well known in his lifetime for his historical paintings and lithographs of the English Royal Family, while her sister Adelaide Agnes painted genre and flower studies. Helena's work has never had quite the recognition it deserves, for her attractive studies of rural life are often better than many of those painted by some of her con-temporaries working in the same genre. She exhibited at the Royal Academy and all the other major galleries from 1881 to 1902, occasionally taking time off from her exhibition work to illustrate children's books. She died in London in November 1909.

Her two watercolours, *A Quiet Corner* and *Messmates* are both idealised studies of children and rural life. *A Quiet Corner*, depicting a country child who has stumbled upon a family of rabbits is charming and the artist has added several telling touches of social realism. The most obvious examples are the crumpled hat on the girl's head, worn as if she were unused to wearing a hat, the dusty shoes and the uneven hem of a badly-made dress. The subject is idealised for the rabbits appear quite unconcerned at the arrival of a human, a species which they had every cause to fear. Rabbits were shot by the gentry, snared by poachers and formed the favourite dish of every farm hand in the land.

Helena Maguire's watercolour, *Messmates*, shows a very young child sitting outside a country cottage, surrounded by family pets who are helping her finish her meal. It is a domestic scene which might have been painted by Landseer, whose paintings of animals did much to establish a vogue for animal subjects.

The child lives in a labourer's cottage, a building that had more than its fair share of shortcomings. Until the middle of the nineteenth century the floor would have been earthen, generally made filthy by the trodden-in litter from the courtyard. In addition, there was no piped water and only primitive sanitation. Roses and wisteria might well grow up the front of such a house but these were merely cosmetic.

A Quiet Corner (left)   *Messmates* (right)
Courtesy The Priory Gallery

CHARLES GREGORY

1849-1920

Born in London on 24 March 1849, Charles Gregory received his art education at the Royal Academy Schools. He began exhibiting in 1873, and later showed at the Royal Academy from 1877 to 1897. A genre and historical watercolour artist as well as an illustrator, his work was often rather sentimental but changed in character slightly when he moved to Surrey in 1892. This was long after Birket Foster and Helen Allingham had settled there, a move which had attracted other artists to the area.

Before the coming of the railways, artists had travelled deep into the heart of rural Britain, painting the country-side and its inhabitants with all the wide-eyed wonder of a tourist in foreign parts. The railways made the country-side accessible and some artists, such as the many who settled in Surrey, then realised that there were plenty of rural subjects available to them locally.

In Surrey 40 per cent of the land was owned by wealthy people not greatly interested in farming and so the painters' subject matter began to change. Instead of portraying simple rustics living in picturesque hovels, the artists now painted riverside scenes and woodland walks. The people inhabiting these pictures were also different, their clothing reflecting the influence of the town rather than the country.

Gregory's painting, *Near Elstead, Surrey* is an example of this new departure. Elstead was, and still is, a quaint village on the River Wey that has a fourteenth-century church, a five-arched bridge and the ruins of Waverley Abbey nearby – the inspiration for Sir Walter Scott's novel, *Waverley*. Although it did not have a deeply rural feeling, there was still enough to attract most painters.

Gregory's painting of its outskirts was a highly successful effort to capture the essence of a semi-rural village, packed with enough detail to occupy the viewer's attention for some time. We see a mother consulting her shopping list as she walks along the tow path with her two young children, the young angler on the river bank, another figure on the bridge, and the background houses which are more urban than rural. The gentle use of warm colours imparts an almost golden glow to the picture, which is an example of a fine craftsman at work.

Charles Gregory ended his days at Marlow-on-Thames, where he died on 21 October 1920.

Near Elstead, Surrey

Courtesy Bourne Gallery

OTTO THEODORE LEYDE

1835-1897

The nineteenth century saw a large number of foreign artists leaving their own homes to settle in Britain, mainly because it was still the capital of the art world, although the French Impressionists had begun to attract increasing admiration. Among these immigrants was Otto Theodore Leyde, a Prussian born in Westlau in 1835. When he was in his early twenties he came to Britain and settled in Edinburgh where he worked as a lithographer. He painted in oils and watercolours and soon established himself in both fields as a talented genre and landscape artist. Although most of his work was exhibited at the major Scottish galleries, it was also accepted for exhibition at the Royal Academy and a number of prestigious London galleries.

Leyde's lovely watercolour, *Happy as the Day is Long*, shows a lonely Scottish beach with two fisher girls bringing back their catch of shellfish. In another fish basket they are carrying a jolly, rosy-faced baby. Executed in such a way that one can almost smell the salty tang on the wind which sends the clouds rolling across the sky, it is a masterly example of 'mood' painting. There are a number of thoughtful touches such as the way the catch has been covered by seaweed to keep it fresh, and the short shadow falls across the sand telling us it is morning.

It was painted at a time when the Victorian genre artists had begun to realise that the seaside offered as much in the way of subject matter as did the conventional rural scene. They painted all the trappings of coastal life, finding much to inspire them, such as an old beached ketch, a fisherman sitting outside his wooden hut contemplating his nets drying on the pebbles before him, or a wreck lying in the shallows, its broken spars standing starkly against the skyline.

The country child, previously wandering among flowers, was now to be seen adorning a beach, or playing with friends or parents. It is worth noting that the beaches in most British paintings of coastal scenes are nearly always deserted, whereas those painted by the French Impressionists are often crowded with people. The sea herself as well as her beaches was also favoured as subject matter and the eighteenth and nineteenth centuries produced many maritime paintings of ships before the wind in full sail, or in the process of going down in mountainous seas. Such variety in the content of maritime paintings gave the Victorians much pleasure as well as lending scope for inherently dramatic pieces – a sharp contrast with the tranquil tenor of most rural scenes.

Happy as the Day is Long
Courtesy Bourne Gallery

WILLIAM HENRY HUNT

1790-1864

As a watercolour artist, William Henry Hunt towers above most of his contemporaries for the sheer truthfulness of his art and his wonderful technique, whether he was painting still-life or a landscape, or one of his famous rustic figures. His work was notable for the light and depth in his scenes and for the rich colours he achieved by a process of his own creation, in which he laid down a base of Chinese White and then applied one rich colour over another giving the finished painting a life-like texture.

Born on 28 March 1790, Hunt's career as an artist was launched by a sad accident of fate. Because of a deformity of his legs which made it difficult for him to walk, his parents decided that the only course open to him was to become an artist. Accordingly, they put him into the care of John Varley who had taught many well-known artists, including David Cox.

Some art historians have regretted that Hunt eventually gave up landscape painting and concentrated instead on still-life and rustic figures. While it is true that his landscapes were remarkable examples of the genre, his work in other areas shows the same mastery of his craft.

Hunt's *A Rustic Beauty* belongs to his large gallery of rural characters, in this case a young country girl. It is indicative of his honesty as an artist that he did not pose her against some attractive background but chose instead to place her in an old shed, full of brushwood and miscellaneous bits and pieces. He devoted as much loving care to painting these oddments as he did to his model. Hunt was well-known for his empathy with the rural characters he painted, which is reflected in the way the girl smiles back at us from the picture with the quiet assurance of someone completely at ease with the painter.

She was, in all probability, a farm servant who would have been hired by the year and given a fixed wage plus board and lodgings. In exchange, she was expected to do all manner of things, ranging from cooking the master's breakfast and carrying out dozens of household chores to tending the chickens and taking the cattle out to graze.

For the unmarried country girl, the choices were few. She could either work in the fields or the house, or be trained from a very young age to go into one of the rural cottage industries such as lace-making or straw plaiting. None of the alternatives gave her much of a future.

A Rustic Beauty
Courtesy Bourne Gallery

SAMUEL McCLOY

1831-1904

Samuel McCloy was an Irish painter, born in Lisburn, Ireland on 13 March 1831. He taught at the Waterford School of Art after serving an apprenticeship with a firm of Belfast engravers. McCloy came to England and began exhibiting from 1875-81. On his arrival in London he continued to show at all the major galleries, except the Royal Academy where, surprisingly, he exhibited only one picture, *The Haunt of Meditation*. He died in Balham, London on 4 October 1904. A figure, flower and genre painter, he sometimes dropped the 'loy' from his signature to form a monogram.

In common with many other Victorian artists he was fond of giving his pictures arch titles such as *Caught in the Net*, *Two Wee Playmates* and *It Won't Come Right*. However, this foible in no way detracts from the quality of his work. Examples of his painting can be found in the Victoria and Albert Museum and the Belfast Gallery.

His watercolour, *A Surgical Operation* is an amusing little study of a young girl who seems to be trying to extract a thorn from the finger of one of her companions, while the other looks on. It is a pleasing genre painting and less overworked than some of his other pieces. It was executed with a careful eye for detail – McCloy shows the girl's lock of falling hair as she bends over the patient's finger; the varying expressions of amusement, concentration and apprehension are also nicely caught.

The two boys in the picture are wearing knickerbockers. These made their first appearance after George Cruikshank illustrated Washington Irving's *History of New York* (1809), which he wrote under the pseudonym 'Knickerbocker'. His illustrations for this book showing seventeenth-century Dutch settlers wearing a similar type of trouser are said to have started the vogue.

Knickerbocker trousers may not have been the most attractive items of clothing for a boy to wear, but they were quite staid after some of the previous fashions for boys. (See page 16.) Another popular outfit was the sailor suit, but both these and the knickerbockers were mild trials when set beside that ultimate Victorian horror – the Norfolk suit. This had appeared in 1880 and had been designed for gentlemen going shooting or for long walks. Looking thoroughly out of place on a child, it was yet another attempt by the Victorian mother to make her son 'a little man'. In general, then, Victorian children had to be long-suffering with regard to their clothes which were scaled-down versions of adult attire.

A Surgical Operation

Courtesy Anthony Mitchell, Fine Paintings

BENJAMIN D. SIGMUND

Flourished 1880-1903

Like many late Victorian artists, Benjamin Sigmund found that the coming of the railways opened up areas of the countryside which previously could only be reached with the greatest difficulty. This enabled much of his work to be painted in areas as far apart as Devon and Cornwall, Wales and Berkshire, as well as in his native county of Buckinghamshire, where he lived at East Burnham, near Slough. A landscape and genre painter who exhibited at the Royal Academy from 1880 to 1903, he also produced two illustrated books, *By the Sea Shore* and *Reeds and Grasses*, which were both published in 1888. Like many artists, his work varied in quality.

He was a painter who always worked outdoors and could therefore be called a *plein air* artist. This term, applied to much of the work of the French Impressionists, referred to an artist who pitched his easel in a field or garden and painted there from sketch to finished watercolour in order to catch the true feeling of the outdoor scene. In contrast, most other artists did their finished work in the studio where it was not possible to achieve the same effect.

Benjamin Sigmund's watercolour, *A Day by the River*, shows him at his best, painting in a tightly controlled manner. It is a charming study of three young children sitting on a bank, watching some swans. The trees are in full leaf and the meadow in which the children sit is ablaze with soap-wort, buttercups and daisies. Perhaps the children are out for a stroll in their Sunday best as they look so smart.

Sigmund shows a marvellous control of colour, with the red of the little girl's shawl making an immediate focal point. The watercolour's great merit is the creation of the tranquil atmosphere of an English summer's day in the country, so vivid that one can almost hear the gentle hum of insects. Sigmund's feeling for the quality of light peculiar to the English countryside is also remarkable and is something which could only have been achieved by an artist painting directly from nature.

Nineteenth-century genre artists painting a rural scene usually chose to portray country children quietly enjoying themselves in idyllic surroundings. Despite all the social documents which give an appalling picture of the hardships such children often endured, these artists were not falsifying the facts for the sake of a pretty picture. Country children often enjoyed themselves, though their pleasures were simple ones. They skipped and played marbles, just as children did in the town, or trundled their iron hoops down the village street. When the weather was fine, they picked flowers or blackberries or sloes for Mama to make wine. They went for walks taking in the beauties of the countryside which they could appreciate far more than any urban dwellers, whose eyes had not been trained to take in all they saw on the way.

A Day by the River

Courtesy Anthony Mitchell, Fine Paintings

HENRY JAMES JOHNSTONE

1835-1907

Most Victorian artists confined their travels to the Continent but Henry James Johnstone journeyed both to Australia and America. He finally came home and settled in London where he died in 1907.

He was born in Birmingham in 1835 and does not seem to have painted many watercolours until he went to Australia in 1853. There, he established a photographic business in Melbourne and painted two watercolours of the Murray River. Twenty years later he went to America, where he stayed for seven years before returning to England in 1880. Johnstone lived first at Marlow, Buckinghamshire and then later in Wadhurst, Sussex. He began exhibiting at all the major galleries from 1884 and often showed at the Royal Academy.

Johnstone was a genre artist of considerable ability. His subject matter was often potentially sentimental but treated in such a realistic, earthy manner as to remove the possibility of criticism.

His watercolour, *Sorry, Boy – None to Spare* is an example of the realism Johnstone was capable of applying to his subject. His young boy having his mid-day meal on a rough-hewn bench after a morning in the fields is not an idealised country lad. This boy's trousers are spattered with mud from the fields and he is wearing boots fit only for the dustbin. He is in a yard, a dumping ground for an old broom head, a well-worn scrubbing brush and a wiping-up cloth lying beside a bucket.

Neither has there been any marked attempt to play on the viewer's sympathy by making the dog or boy look particularly appealing. This watercolour is indeed a superbly executed piece of social realism.

The dog was most unlikely to be given any left-overs. The boy's diet was bread and weak tea made from leaves that had probably been used more than once. This would be supplemented with bread smeared with dripping, home-grown vegetables and a little bacon and cheese, facts that were established in a dietary survey carried out in 1863. Milk was not readily available as any spare was given to the family pig. In really bad times bread was made from what was called 'crammings', the residue left after the flour and bran had been extracted. This was supplemented by turnips and swedes. As for tea, this was often brewed from burnt crusts of bread.

The family was lucky if it saw butcher's meat more than twice a week. The one thing that made life tolerable was the family pig which sustained them throughout much of the year with a plentiful supply of pork and bacon. This rural 'perk' meant that the farm labourer and his family were far better off than the urban poor.

Sorry, Boy – None to Spare
Courtesy The Priory Gallery

HENRY MEYNELL RHEAM

1859-1920

A genre painter born in Birkenhead on 13 January 1859, Henry Meynell Rheam studied in Germany and Paris before returning to England. He exhibited at all the major galleries including the Royal Academy from 1887, a period when many artists were abandoning the cities for the coast and countryside.

Joining in the general migration, Rheam went to live in Polperro, Cornwall, only to move on shortly afterwards to the small fishing village of Newlyn, where a colony of painters had established the Newlyn School of Artists. However, Rheam's reason for settling there had nothing to do with art. Hearing that he was an excellent batsman, the local cricket team persuaded him to come and live in Newlyn hoping thus to strengthen their team in the annual match against the artists of St Ives! Once there, Rheam not surprisingly became a member of the Newlyn School of Artists.

The first painter to arrive in Newlyn had been Walter Langley, a Birmingham artist who went there in 1882 and was joined two years later by Stanhope Forbes. More than anyone else, Forbes was to be responsible for establishing the reputation of the Newlyn School. Indeed, when his masterpiece, *A Fish Sale on a Cornish Beach*, created a sensation on its showing at the Royal Academy in 1885, serious critical attention was first attracted to the School. By 1900 many of the artists had left, yet one may still view the Newlyn School as a coda to the great age of Victorian painting.

Rheam's watercolour, *The Music Lesson*, shows a young fisherman playing the flute for a small but attentive audience of two little girls sitting in an outhouse full of nets and fishermen's tackle. Afterwards, the two girls will run back to their cosy-looking, whitewashed cottages which were always kept spotlessly clean.

This is not to say that the life led by Rheam's two little girls was an easy one. In a bad year, the hauls of fish could be pitifully small, and a family reduced to near starvation. The fishermen were engaged in a hazardous occupation and, inevitably, children sometimes heard the sad news that their father had been drowned at sea.

Despite all this, Newlyn was a contented, God-fearing fishing community that got on well with the artists who had come into their midst. The children seemed equally happy and grew up with little or no desire to leave Newlyn for the bright lights of nearby Penzance. (See also page 56.)

The Music Lesson
Courtesy The Priory Gallery

CARLTON ALFRED SMITH

1853-1946

Carlton Alfred Smith often painted 'mood' pieces executed in such a realistic manner as to give an imaginative viewer the feeling of having stepped back in time.

His painting, *Waiting For Playmates*, shown on the back cover, is an excellent example of his work. The little girl, in blue cotton dress and pink pinafore, sits on an empty beach, hoping for some other children to appear and play. Placing the child to the left of the drawing emphasises her loneliness since the remaining space is thus given over to depicting a large expanse of beach, deserted except for a few gulls and a distant figure, perhaps the child's mother. The watercolour is a superb example of a genre painting with under-stated subject.

After School Hours is another fine instance of Carlton Smith's work where the subject is treated in a more straightforward manner. The painting is rich in detail, and the artist has carefully balanced the blue of the girl's dress with the blue of the sky reflected in the water. The boy is wearing a smock, an all-weather garment. The water jug had probably been brought along to hold the bait.

The two children in the picture having time to indulge in this form of leisure after school hours implies that the painting was done after the 1875 Education Act. This Act imposed full-time attendance on all country children between the ages of five and ten and part-time attendance until the age of fourteen. It effectively put a stop to the hitherto common practice of forcing children to work all day in the fields when they should have been at school, and was the beginning of some long overdue reforms.

For the children in Carlton Smith's watercolour, the Act did something more than provide the chance for a better education; now they were free to enjoy such pleasant pastimes as fishing instead of being forced to work in the fields until dusk.

Carlton Smith was born on 27 August 1853, the son of a steel engraver. Educated in France, he received his art training at the famous Slade School in London. Afterwards he worked as a lithographer for several years before deciding finally that his true *métier* was painting, a career in which he was so successful that he was exhibiting regularly at the Royal Academy by the time he was twenty-six. He lived in London, where he died in 1946.

After School Hours
Courtesy The Priory Gallery

MYLES BIRKET FOSTER

1825-1899

A watercolour artist of considerable repute, Myles Birket Foster's work has always been popular. A genre artist who delighted in painting sunny, rural scenes peopled by rustic children and cheerful-looking farm workers, his pictures capture all that was best in the life of the agricultural communities of Britain.

Birket Foster started off his professional career as an engraver, and then took to book illustration before turning seriously to watercolour painting. From the very beginning, his watercolours were exhibited by all the major galleries, where dealers scrambled to buy them.

He left London in 1861 and settled in Witley, Surrey, from where he went on working trips abroad. A major excursion was to Venice, where he painted a series of commissioned scenes. He died in Weybridge, Surrey, on 27 March 1899.

His watercolour, *The Bird's Nest*, was first shown to the public in 1862 at the Summer Exhibition of the Royal Society of Painters of Watercolours, together with seven other watercolours, including two painted on the Isle of Wight. This fine example of his work depicts a shepherd boy taking a rest from tending his flock to show his young friend a blackbird's nest and some eggs that have come from a variety of other birds, including a starling, hedge sparrow and thrush. Obviously, they are a secret cache the boy has collected over a period of time. As with all Birket Foster's work, the painting is notable for its delicacy and fine finish.

The shepherd boy's interest in bird life was not one shared by the Victorian farmer, who saw birds as an evil to be wiped out by whatever means he could find. As sparrows were the worst offenders when it came to eating newly-sown corn, sparrow-catching clubs were formed, financially supported by the farmers. Children acted as bird scarers for a few coppers a day. Armed with a rattle or a spade and bucket to bang, they reported for work at dawn and stayed in the fields until dusk. The farmers refused to allow two boys to work together as they knew they would spend all their time playing, so the bird scarer's job was a lonely one.

The Bird's Nest

Courtesy Phillips

WILLIAM LUCAS

1840-1895

Born in London in 1840, William Lucas was already an accomplished artist by the age of sixteen, when his first work was shown at the Royal Academy. Specialising in portrait and figure paintings, he eventually received enough favourable comment to be invited to become an Associate of the New Society of Artists; at this point he was only twenty-four. Suddenly, at the age of thirty-seven, he was struck down by ill-health and his promising career as a painter was permanently blighted. Lucas was forced to give up painting and turn instead to the less demanding field of lithography. Although he painted a large number of rural scenes, he always lived in London, where he died in 1895. His early promise was never really fulfilled but he still managed to leave one hundred and thirty watercolours, many of them of considerable merit.

He came from an artistic family. His father was John Lucas (1807-74), a famous portrait painter, who had numbered among his sitters the Prince Consort and the Duke of Wellington. His brother John Templeton Lucas (1836-80) was a frequent exhibitor at the Royal Academy. His cousin John Seymour Lucas (1849-1923) was a well-known Royal Academician, whose painting, *After Culloden, Rebel Hunting*, was bought by the Chantrey Bequest, created for 'the purchase of works of fine art of the highest merit'.

William Lucas's watercolour, *The Rose Pickers*, is worthy of study for the subtle juxtaposition of colours.

The various shades of green act as a background for the three different colours used for the clothing, drawing the eye to the picture's focal point – the three children picking wild roses. The almost perpendicular and parallel lines of the primitive and long-disused horse-drawn roller also draw attention to the same area.

As the children are not dressed in the sort of clothing one might expect of a farmer's offspring, it is likely that they come from the solid-looking house seen to the right of the picture and are from a well-to-do family. The complete absence of sheep, cows or cornfields in the background suggests that this is not an agricultural area but close to a town. The small cloth laid on the ground is for wrapping up the roses that are being prepared either as a pot-pourri, or for pressing between the pages of a book, two popular hobbies in Victorian times.

The picture certainly does not show a Sunday, when children from well-to-do families were regular attenders at church or morning Sunday school. The rest of the day was often spent reading carefully selected 'improving' books or mawkish tales in which the little hero or heroine invariably expired at a tender age – a salutary reminder to all their young readers that Death was never far away. Indeed, the Victorian stress on religion and morality, even if often only skin deep, would make such unseemly scrambling about on a Sunday for such children quite unthinkable.

The Rose Pickers
Courtesy J. Collins & Son

GEORGE LAWRENCE BULLEID

1858-1933

Born in Glastonbury on 24 April 1858, the son of a local solicitor, George Lawrence Bulleid was a Victorian artist who painted equally well in both oil and watercolours. He began exhibiting in 1888, and continued to do so until his death in 1933. His work consisted almost entirely of figures, still-life and mythological subjects, the latter being extremely popular with the Victorian public. Bulleid's mythological paintings have a classic charm which lifts them above the work of many other nineteenth-century artists whose pictures tend to be over-blown and heavy-handed. He exhibited two hundred and twenty-six pictures in total, fourteen of them at the Royal Academy.

Bulleid's *The Pink Bonnet* is an unaffected portrait study. He has placed his subject against a dark colour which serves as an ideal background for the beautiful young country girl with her golden hair and blue eyes, complementing the pink sun bonnet she is wearing.

In the 1880s, when Bulleid's picture was probably painted, the country girl still wore the traditional sunbonnet made from linen or calico, with a protective neck flap, a piece of millinery we see time and time again in Victorian paintings of the rural scene. A country girl working on the land was unaffected by any of the constantly changing styles in millinery but this did not apply to a young woman belonging to the gentry who had the time and money to wear something more becoming. Even then, she confined herself almost entirely to wearing some form of bonnet, which was one of the most popular types of headgear in the 1840s and continued to be so until well into the late nineteenth, even twentieth century. The merit of the bonnet for the country wearer was the simplicity of its design which, however much it varied, never looked out of place in the country.

Indeed, the style of the bonnet seemed to change with every decade. In the 1850s it was placed far back on the head, showing the hair to the crown and decorated with artificial flowers. The brims were often merged with the crown of the hat from which bonnet strings were attached, bringing the rim down to frame the face.

In the following decade the 'spoon' bonnet appeared. This style had a narrow brim on each side which rose upwards in the front into a spoon shape in which nestled an artificial flower.

The 1870s saw the arrival of the serrated straw bonnet with a *bavolet*, a form of curtain at the back not unlike the sun bonnet's neck flap.

Throughout the 1880s and 1890s the bonnet shape began to change into something more like a hat in appearance, with an excessive use of ribbons and artificial flowers.

The Pink Bonnet
Courtesy Bourne Gallery

WILLIAM STEPHEN COLEMAN

1829-1904

William Stephen Coleman often painted in the manner of Birket Foster. Born in Horsham, Sussex, in 1829, the son of a physician, he trained to enter the medical profession as a surgeon, before his keen interest in nature drew him to painting. His work embraced a wide subject area ranging from pastoral and genre scenes to neo-classical figures which he painted in an attempt to emulate the success of another artist, Albert Moore. (Moore's paintings of neo-classical figures became popular with the public after they had been admired by Whistler.)

In addition, he worked in pastels and oils as well as being an engraver and a popular illustrator of books, mostly on natural history, including *Common Objects of the Country* (1858), *Our Woodlands, Heaths and Hedges* (1859) and *British Butterflies* (1860), both of which ran through several editions. These were followed by *British Birds' Eggs and Nests* and *Sketches in Natural History*, published in 1861.

In 1869 Coleman decided to experiment with pottery decoration. His work in this field was so successful that in 1871 he was asked to establish The Minton Art Pottery Studio in Kensington Gore where he designed a large number of their tiles.

His busy life came to an end at his home at 11 Hamilton Gardens, St John's Wood on 22 March 1904. In the same year a posthumous exhibition of some of his figure subjects, landscapes and decorative panels was held at the Modern Galleries in New Bond Street. It was a fitting tribute to a particularly talented artist whose work ranks highly among nineteenth century genre artists. One of his watercolours showing a girl with a basket of coral can be seen at the Bethnal Green Museum of Childhood in London.

His watercolour, *The Primrose Gatherers*, differs from those of his works done after the manner of Birket Foster; the style is more free and Impressionistic, although equally appealing in its treatment. While the girl holding the basket wears the traditional country bonnet and pinafore over her dress, the other's hat and dress seem more fashionable – perhaps she is a visiting relative come to the country by means of the newly instituted railways.

The Primrose Gatherers
Courtesy The Priory Gallery

AUGUSTUS EDWARD MULREADY

Flourished 1863-1905

Victorians who were fond of painting children drew their inspiration from two main sources. One was the countryside, where they found children of humble farming folk who they portrayed in a wide variety of charming rural situations. The other source was the streets of London, where they found equally rewarding subjects in the ragged urchins whose struggle for survival provided a rich variety of material.

These waifs and strays living on the edge of London's underworld were painted in any sort of situation calculated to bring a furtive tear to the eye of the viewer. Pathetic little mites sing carols in the snow, while they watch wistfully through a window the merry-making of their luckier counterparts inside; children beg limping on crutches, or queue with adults for admission to a casual ward where the homeless could find shelter for a couple of nights – such were the scenes which the painter's sympathetic eye captured in oils or watercolour.

One of the best of these artists was Augustus Edward Mulready, who painted in both oils and watercolour and was a member of what was known as the 'Cranbrook Group' formed by a number of well-known artists living near Cranbrook in Kent. He was a powerful painter whose pictures of the juvenile London poor give us a valuable pictorial record of Victorian street life.

His watercolour *Sympathy – A Scene on Waterloo Bridge*, shows a ragged young street musician consoling an equally pathetic-looking little girl. There is a companion picture in the London Museum entitled, *A London Crossing Sweeper and a Flower Girl*, in which Mulready has used a similar view of the Thames in the background.

If Mulready's waifs and strays seem sentimentally depicted, they were nevertheless very much part of the grim reality of Victorian street life. Emerging every morning from the cellars and archways where they slept, the children came on to the streets where they tried to survive as crossing sweepers, thieves, pickpockets or beggars, facing the daily risk of being caught and led away by some stern custodian of the law to a House of Correction. It was the world of Dickens's *Oliver Twist* (1838), except that, in life, the likelihood of rescue by some kind benefactor was remote. But it is Gustave Dore's searing illustrations in *London*, published in 1872, which convey as the works of no other artist have done the wretched quality of London's low life.

Sympathy –
A Scene on Waterloo Bridge
Courtesy Bourne Gallery

CHARLES EDWARD WILSON

1854-1936

The county of Surrey was a kind of Mecca for the large number of Victorian artists who settled there, among them Myles Birket Foster, Helen Allingham and Charles Edward Wilson who went to live in Godalming in 1896. It was here that Wilson painted most of his major works.

Born at Whitwell, Nottinghamshire, in 1854, he began studying art at the early age of eight. After attending the Sheffield School of Art, Wilson went on to win a number of competitions and was twice awarded a silver medal by the South Kensington Museum. After he had been asked to prepare an album of drawings for the Prince of Wales, he went to Paris to work for the well known *Journal L'Art*.

During the early part of his professional career he shared a cottage in Surrey with Carlton Alfred Smith. Their mutual love of the countryside and complete agreement on how to develop their watercolour technique led to an apparent similarity in both the subject matter and style of their work.

In 1891 he began exhibiting at all the major galleries, including the Walker Gallery in Liverpool. At the Royal Academy he had one hundred pictures accepted for viewing – an incredible number. In 1926 cataracts in both eyes forced him to give up painting until, in 1936, he underwent an operation which restored his sight. His last-known address was at Addiscombe, Surrey, where he lived until his death in 1936.

Typical examples of his oeuvre include *Fetching Water*, showing a little girl filling a bucket from a water barrel, *A Mute Appeal* depicting a dog begging in front of its young mistress who is eating from a bowl standing in a doorway and *The Bird's Nest*, also showing a girl standing in a doorway, with a nest in one hand and a bird's egg in the other.

Wilson's scenes, often of young rustic children, were clearly painted with a great deal of affection. But, as was true for nearly all Victorian artists, he viewed his subjects with the eye of the city dweller, and failed to observe the harsher aspects of rural life. Not that country pleasures did not exist, especially if one were still too young to be sent out to work. Children enjoyed the spring and summertime when they could play outside and escape the general overcrowding of the average country cottage. Country children were surrounded by wholesome air, by fields and hedgerows and could take part in many colourful fairs and festivals, while their urban counterparts were forced to spend their summers wandering the grimy streets.

Something of the idyllic life a country child could live was captured by Wilson in his charming watercolour, *The Picnic*, where a girl shares an outdoor lunch with her younger sibling. As it is summer, she is probably looking after him while their mother is helping in the fields.

The Picnic
Courtesy The Priory Gallery

LIONEL PERCY SMYTHE and HENRY CHARLES FOX

1839-1918   Flourished 1879-1913

The watercolour, *Springtime*, is unusual in that it was painted by two artists. This practice was not uncommon among Victorian artists, if it was felt that another hand working on the painting might strengthen its value, both artistically and commercially. Often the end result was better than might have been expected. In this piece the figures were painted by Lionel Percy Smythe while the background was executed by Henry Charles Fox.

Lionel Percy Smythe, who was born in London on 4 September 1839, is the better-known artist. He was a highly-talented landscape and genre painter who specialised in rustic figures, which were always executed in delicate colours. Smythe was influenced by John William North.

Later in his life, Smythe went to live in Wimereux in the Pas de Calais, where he continued to work until his death on 10 July 1918.

Henry Charles Fox was a painter of landscape and genre subjects. Born in London in 1860, he exhibited at the Royal Academy from 1879 to 1902, but continued to exhibit at other galleries right up until 1913. Thereafter little is known about him, although we do know that in 1922 he was still alive and living at Kingston-on-Thames. The backgrounds in his paintings were generally more effective than his figures which is probably why he collaborated here with Smythe. Their watercolour, *Springtime*, shows just how well the talents of two artists can come together to create an artistically successful watercolour. Notice how the subtle tints used on Smythe's little girls are effectively contrasted against the darker hues of Fox's backgrounds.

The children in the picture had probably been sent off to occupy themselves in the woods with their dog, whom one of the girls has recently adorned with a garland of flowers. The preservation of this lovely woodland was due to the efforts of far-off Londoners, whose untiring protests at the continual clearance of thousands upon thousands of wooded acres for agricultural purposes finally led to the conservation of the remaining forests from 1870 onwards.

Springtime
Courtesy Bourne Gallery

ARTHUR CLAUDE STRACHAN

Exhibited 1885–1932

A well-known painter of landscapes and country cottages, Arthur Claude Strachan was born in Edinburgh in 1865. His subject matter, country cottages whose gardens always abounded with flowers in full bloom, inevitably reminds one of Henry Allingham's work, although the style of his treatment is a little broader. After receiving his art training in Liverpool, Strachan began exhibiting at most of the London and provincial galleries from 1885, and continued to do so regularly up to 1932. As he lived in a number of different countries, it is sometimes difficult to pinpoint the exact location of some of his scenes. His last known address was in Glasgow, where he was living in 1929.

Looking at *The Puppy*, one can understand why Victorian artists derived so much pleasure from painting country cottages. This picture epitomises everyone's dream of the perfect cottage, hemmed in with flowers, leaded window panes reflecting the light of a summer day, the garden ablaze with the colours of hollyhocks, foxglove, sweet william and marguerites. The small girl in pinafore and sun-bonnet intent on watching her puppy playing with his bone, complete the picture. It is a painting which shows very clearly the artist's genuine love for the English countryside.

Unlike most of the early Victorian cottages made from wattle and daub, this one is built of brick. The social reformers had been pleading for this form of construction for years, but had only begun to see their wishes realised after 1850, when a tax on bricks was removed. Even then the building speculators were slow to respond, deterred by the knowledge that a labourer on low wages was unlikely to pay more for his improved accommodation than the shilling or so weekly rent that was normally due.

Two events changed the situation: one was mechanisation which enabled the production of cheap bricks; the other was the general exodus from the land which had started in the 1870s and reached its peak with the coming of the railways. These two events, occurring at much the same time, had led to falling rents. This meant that, for the first time in his life, a labourer could pick and choose from a large selection of houses whenever he wanted to move. The speculator was forced to knock down many old buildings and construct new ones from brick.

Regrettably, the building boom was short lived. By the turn of the century land had no longer become easily available for the speculator to buy, building materials were suddenly less obtainable and timber difficult to find, since many wooded places had become conservation areas.

The Puppy
Courtesy The Priory Gallery

MINNIE JANE HARDMAN

Born 1867

Although many thousands of watercolours had been produced by the end of the 1800s, the public had not grown tired of the traditional watercolours of the rural scene. These gave an idyllic picture of country life, with the emphasis often on happy children wandering among fields and meadows where wild flowers always seemed to grow. Indeed, the public still wanted that type of picture and there were still many artists who could satisfy the demand.

Among these artists, who also specialised in painting children, were many women. Some of the notable names in this field were Jessica Haylar (1858-1940) and her sister Mary (flourished 1880-85) who painted miniatures of children, Eleanor Fortesque Brickdale (1871-1945) who was also a stained-glass artist, responsible for designing some of the windows for Bristol Cathedral, Elizabeth Stanhope Forbes (1859-1912) who founded the famous Newlyn Art School with her husband, Stanhope Forbes, and the renowned watercolour artist and illustrator, Kate Greenaway (1844-1901) whose work influenced many people to dress their children in 'Kate Greenaway' costume. Among the other artists working in this field must be included Minnie Jane Hardman.

A genre, portrait and flower painter, Minnie Hardman's work remained unnoticed by the critics until she began exhibiting at the Royal Academy in 1900. Her paintings are notable for their delicacy, which sometimes matched that of her more eminent colleagues working in the genre. *Picking Buttercups* has a charming air of innocence about it. As a very late Victorian painter she might well have been lured into tackling her subject with a different approach, one more in line with some of the experimental methods of artists beginning to explore new techniques. Instead, her work remained rooted in the old traditions of watercolour painting.

Picking Buttercups is a highly accomplished piece. By the application of transparent watercolour washes to the trees and field, she uses the white of the paper to give an added brightness to her colours. The two girls are painted more opaquely which immediately makes them the focal point. Had she chosen to depict them in the same style, they would have merged into the background.

The popularity of such paintings was not due solely to the fact that they made attractive pictures to hang on the wall, but also to the fact that they struck a responsive chord with the Victorians, who loved to pick flowers themselves. The Victorians had a mania for natural history in all its forms, a passionate interest which led them to collect insects, butterflies, sea shells. fossils, birds' eggs, and, of course, wild flowers.

Picking Buttercups
Courtesy The Priory Gallery

MARY WINEFRIDE FREEMAN

Flourished 1895–1912

Mary Winefride Freeman exhibited at the Royal Academy between 1895 and 1912. Hers was a vigorous style and one which would have been well-suited to book illustration, though there is no evidence that she ever undertook this sort of work. Originally a Londoner, she also lived in Falmouth and Bushey, Hertfordshire, where she did much of her painting, and her work was always well represented at all the major galleries.

Although she could lay no claim to having belonged to the famous Newlyn School of Artists, Mary Winefride Freeman did live and work there briefly in 1897, before making another move, this time to Brighton, returning later to Penzance.

Hurry Up! is full of vitality. Painted in Old Paul's Hill, Newlyn, it may well have been inspired by the work of a well-known Newlyn artist, Percy Craft whose *Heva, Heva!* was painted in 1888.

Craft's painting deals with one of the important events in the lives of the local fishermen. Great shoals of pilchards arrived at Newlyn Bay in the late summer or early autumn, and were spotted by a look-out whose call 'Heva! Heva!' summoned the fishermen from their cottages and sent them scurrying down to their boats to catch the huge quantities of pilchards gathering in Mount Bay. The word 'Heva' is an old Cornish one meaning in this context 'They're swarming!' The look-outs were called 'Huers'.

Percy Craft's picture shows fishermen passing round word of the arrival of the pilchards and Mary Freeman's painting depicts a boy running down the hill, calling out to everyone to hurry down to the bay. It says much for her work that her handling of the subject is better than Craft's, whose treatment of the fishermen and village folk is rather wooden, whereas Freeman's running boy conveys a wonderful sense of movement.

Newlyn would have attracted any painter with its compact little community of fisherfolk whose livelihood was governed by the mackerel, pilchard and herring season, when the men would be out in the Atlantic for as long as three months before returning home.

It was a wonderful period not only for the artists at Newlyn, but also for the fisherfolk, who found themselves gaining a form of immortality, their faces painted on paper and canvas for posterity. But, sadly, the great days when millions of pilchards were hauled in soon passed. The pilchards and mackerel went to other waters and one by one the painters left, leaving the fishermen to the mercy of the tourists.

Hurry Up!
Courtesy Fine-Lines (Fine Art)

ALICE SQUIRE

1840-1936

Alice Squire was a landscape artist and genre painter who had been born early enough to see the great days of William Turner and David Cox. Dying at the age of ninety-six, she survived well beyond the age of Picasso's cubism – an enormous contrast to the great Romantic tradition of watercolour painting in which she had been brought up.

Her own work was in the popular style of its time; it was sentimental and generally aimed to appeal to the layman rather than the critic, while never departing from that solid craftsmanship common to nearly all the Victorian artists. She began exhibiting at the age of twenty-four and, nine years later, became a regular contributor to the Royal Academy, where her work continued to be shown until 1893.

Wash Day is a charming genre watercolour of a young country mother putting some of her washing out to dry on the grass with the assistance of her little daughter. Various influences appear to be at work here. The mother could have been a Pre-Raphaelite figure, with her red hair and sensitive face, while the general treatment is rather reminiscent of Helen Allingham's style. In addition, the little flecks of white on the trees and bushes give the impression that a 'pointillist' method was used – a technique in which dots of unmixed colours are so closely juxtaposed that they fuse into a whole when viewed from a distance.

The relationship between mother and child is clearly a close one. This mother was forced to have her child with her all the time, unlike the mother of an upper-class family, who could distance herself from children by means of the nursery and a nanny or governess. However, the great scourge for all mothers was the high mortality rate among young children. Despite the often squalid conditions in which they were brought up, it was, nevertheless, the country children who had the best chance of survival.

The country child was brought up in a household where the mother made her own bread and where local produce and fresh vegetables were used. In marked contrast, one of the scandals of the Victorian age was the way urban shop-keepers adulterated their food. In a survey carried out in 1855, it was found that, amongst many abuses, milk was being watered down by as much as 50 per cent, fruit and vegetables were being contaminated by copper, sugar coloured by the addition of chromate of lead, and alum was being added to bread to make it hold more water and therefore weigh more. Decidedly dangerous as well as dishonest practices!

Wash Day
Courtesy Fine-Lines (Fine Art)

WILLIAM LEE-HANKEY

1869-1952

A major figure in the art world of the late nineteenth and early twentieth century, William Lee-Hankey was one of those rare artists who adapted himself successfully to each medium he chose. An etcher and a painter both in oils and watercolours, as well as an occasional book illustrator, he eventually became the leading British exponent of Impressionism. His work can now be found in many major collections, both in England and abroad.

Lee-Hankey was born on 28 March 1869 in Chester, where he studied in the local school of art before going on to Paris for further studies. He began exhibiting at all the major galleries, including the Royal Academy as well as at the Paris Salon, and other European galleries. A landscape, genre and figure painter, he worked primarily in oils. However, he is an important figure in the field of watercolours, where he introduced a number of new techniques making his work immediately recognisable and setting him apart from the mainstream of Victorian watercolourists. One of his many qualities was his ability to capture his sitter's mood to a degree that one feels one almost knows what they are thinking.

The two examples of his work shown here give an accurate idea of his highly individual style. One can see how his training as an engraver is used to produce a fine and unobtrusive line which combines with tonal qualities to help bring the picture alive.

To judge by the clothing of the young women in the two pictures these people are a little higher up the social scale than those normally featured by painters of the rural scene.

During this period women of all social stratas had one thing in common; their only future lay in marriage. For example, both the two girls in *Sisters* faced an organised but dull future, which had only marginally changed from that of a nicely brought-up girl of the early part of the nineteenth century for whom marriage was the ultimate goal. Even if Lee-Hankey's two girls were eventually to go to university, as a number of young women did in the 1890s, they would still be hampered by the barrier of their sex and prejudice against women. It was difficult for any woman to advance her career unless she had a formidable personality and an iron will.

In *Halcyon Days* only the youngest child would grow up into a more progressive age with a choice of other alternatives.

Sisters (left)   *Halcyon Days* (right)

Courtesy Bourne Gallery   Courtesy The Priory Gallery